HOLY COMMON SENSE

THE LORD'S PRAYER FOR TODAY

HOLY COMMON SENSE

DAVID H. C. READ

ABINGDON PRESS NASHVILLE AND NEW YORK

In Memoriam
HENRY R. LUCE

PREFACE

The present turmoil in the churches and uproar in theology is naturally having its repercussions in the area of personal and public devotion. Already the modern Christian has been in difficulty about his prayers, and now his perplexities are being compounded by radical questions about God and what used to be known as the "supernatural." What can we believe about prayer, either as a personal conversation with a "personal God" or as a ritual act in the tradition of our forefathers?

This book comes from the conviction that it is better to begin with the prayer than the questioning. It starts from the proposition that Christ himself prayed to a "Father in heaven" and clearly instructed his followers to do the same. It assumes that it is never easy to pray in any age, and that modern man—while encountering some peculiar difficulties—needs precisely the same stimulus and can experience the same reality as any of his predecessors.

The Lord's Prayer suffers as a model from the sheer familiarity of its wording. Everyone knows how easy it is to let the words slip out without any real concentration on the meaning. Yet I am convinced that no other prayer can teach us so much about the nature and reality of private and communal devotion. So here is an attempt to focus attention on the actual content of the prayer as we say it, alone or together, in the context of the world we live in today.

The prayer, it has often been remarked, is not original in the sense that it contains thoughts that had never before been expressed. Nor is it specifically "Christian"—since it can be prayed by adherents of any of the great religions. Yet I believe that it can only be fully understood in the light of the gospel, and have therefore linked each phrase closely to the basic content of the New Testament.

I hope that these addresses, originally prepared for the spoken voice, may in printed form offer some little illumination of these hallowed words today, and—above all—be a stimulus to actual praying. For this is certainly our greatest need.

My gratitude goes to all who have given me such incentive in the past, and to those who are keeping this subject before our minds today. And I would also express warm thanks to my secretary, Miss Agnes Dougall, for her skillful and devoted preparation of the manuscript.

DAVID H. C. READ
Madison Avenue Presbyterian Church
New York City

CONTENTS

1. Who Prays to Whom?

This is how you should pray:
  Our Father in heaven . . .

"This is *how* you should pray"—not "*why* you should pray." In this, as in so much else, Jesus Christ shows himself wiser than those who speak in his name today. For a great many of our sermons on prayer are arguments about why we should pray, while the evidence is that most people would rather hear about how it should be done. A recent poll among church members revealed this as the No. 1 topic that they wanted preached about, and I believe this would be true for many who are unconnected with any Christian congregation. It doesn't follow that the kind of sermon we want to hear is necessarily the one that we *should* hear, but in this instance I'm sure the desire is well founded. We need to learn how to pray.

13

I propose, therefore, to examine the model prayer offered by our Lord in response to this need. We shall not interpret the "how" in the sense of what you might call "techniques of prayer." You will notice that, apart from the remark about going into a room by oneself and shutting the door, Jesus was not concerned with the precise way we go about this business. I am not going to spend any time discussing whether, in order to pray, we should kneel down, sit in a chair, stand upright, or—as some cults now recommend—stand on our head in order to meditate and converse with our God. Not does the Bible authorize me to offer some secret formula which will provide, as it were, a hot line to God; or some magic words guaranteed to produce results. The "how" refers to the content of our prayers, what we should actually say when we are attempting to talk with God. This is what our Lord gives us, and one of the most healthful exercises we can use is surely to ponder again the implications of each phrase he used in this model prayer.

Immediately before he gave it he issued a warning—almost as though he guessed that any form of prayer he gave was liable to be misused and turned into a magic incantation to be rattled off as often as possible in order to impress and influence the Almighty. "In your prayers do not go babbling on like the heathen, who imagine that the more

14

they say the more likely they are to be heard." We may be thinking now of the misuse of this prayer by those who rattle it off so many times a day as a religious duty or penance; or of the superstition that impels a man to carry a tiny engraving of the prayer when going on a journey. (There is a machine in the Grand Central Station that offers them for a dime.) We should really be thinking of the number of times we ourselves in the sanctuary have muttered the familiar words without thinking of their meaning, or said them quickly in our private prayers at night with a quite unworthy sense of duty done.

"This is how you should pray." He assumes we will pray and asks for sincerity and attention—at least as much sincerity and attention as we would give in talking to someone in authority on earth. If I were granted an interview by the President and wanted to ask him to attend a special service in my church, I should approach him with respect, concentrate on what I wanted to say, and say it as clearly as possible. I should hardly fling myself on the nearest couch, gabble the words: "Mr. President - will - you - please - come - to - my - church - for - this - very - important - service - good-bye - I'm - going - to - sleep."

"This is how you should pray." Who is doing the praying? I don't believe that this "you" is directed to any special group. If you like, it is dis-

15

ciples he is talking to and this is a prayer for Christians. But Christians are not meant to be a special group. The appeal of Christ is to all men, and this is a universal prayer. Every phrase in it can already be paralleled in the Hebrew of the Old Testament. It comes to us from the Greek and is repeated today in almost every language in the world. Human beings pray. Like laughter and the making of tools this is the sign of our humanity. Man is the animal that laughs, uses tools, and prays.

How? With words. He suggests words for us to use. But surely we know better than that. If modern man is still an animal who prays, he's surely too sophisticated to talk. If prayer is communion with that which is greater than ourselves, we say its highest form—and the only form that can have meaning today—must be an inward dedication, a profound meditation, an opening of ourselves to others in love and service: but not *talk*. Prayer-talk belongs to the childhood of the race, and we have grown beyond it. Thus an effort is being made to redefine prayer for modern man. Bishop Robinson tells us that "prayer is the responsibility to meet others with all I have, to be ready to encounter the unconditional in the conditional, to expect to meet God in the way, not to turn aside from the way." Paul van Buren tells us that in the old days when your neighbor's field suffered from drought you talked to God about it. Today you think hard about

16

his plight and then you go to offer some practical suggestions. That is prayer. Jesus said: "This is how you should pray: Our Father . . ."

The men I have quoted are, of course, perfectly right to remind us that prayer is not a substitute for action, that prayer has dimension for which words are inadequate, that prayer is not a flight from the secular to a supernatural world. They have felt in their bones the irrelevance and irresponsibility of much of our praying in the churches today. They are sick of the weary words and tired expressions and skepticism about the terms we use and the confidence we have in them. But their bold attempt to reshape the faith in secular terms, to redefine prayer so that it will be acceptable to the man who has no God to talk to, runs headlong into this plain fact of Christian history: Jesus both taught and practised "talking to God." "When ye pray, say: Our Father . . ."

Words are, after all, the means of our self-expression. They may be used simply to convey information or to store it in a book. In that case we are talking about something, or someone, as I am now talking to you about prayer and about God. Words pass across from me to you and convey—or do not convey—the thoughts in my mind. But words have another way of expression—literal *self*-expression. In this case I do not simply talk about someone. I talk *to* you. *I* talk to *you*. I am revealing myself to

17

you. You are not just absorbing information. You are being addressed. It is the difference between a boy writing on the wall "John loves Jane" and John telling Jane: "I love you." It is the difference between my saying: "The Bible declares that God loves all men" and saying: "I believe that God loves you." Such words are not just symbols used to carry information. They are vehicles of the spirit. They are alive. It was this that Jesus said, according to the Fourth Gospel: "The words that I speak unto you, they are Spirit, and they are life."

So when we use words, when we say: "Our Father," we are not saying something *about* God, but *to* him. We are expressing ourselves, opening our life and spirit to Another. This is communication—person to person. And this raises immediately the central question of all prayer, which is also the storm center of religious debate in our generation. To whom, or to what are we talking? The real reason why some today are questioning and revising our conception of prayer is that they have ceased to believe that there is anything resembling a personal God to whom we can talk. If there is not, then words of prayer are empty symbols. They bounce back from a secular world like ping-pong balls from the ceiling. We are talking to ourselves.

What the radical theologians are doing is to express quite openly and boldly what many Christians

18

have actually experienced. Which of us has not had our moments of doubt when we wondered if, in fact, there was anybody there? Don't imagine you are the only church member who has felt like this —for a fleeting moment, or even for months under a cloud of doubt and dull confusion. And don't imagine that it is always simple and easy for a pastor when he offers prayer with a person in deep distress; when, for instance, a young mother who has lost her child looks him in the eye, after such prayer, and says: "Do you really believe that God is there?"

This is the real question behind all that is said today about our image of God, all the arguments about how we should talk of him. By all means let us think again about the language we have used to speak of God. There is every reason to heed the warning that what is now called "God-talk" has been too facile and too glib. The traditional formulas of our prayers and our creeds may indeed have died in the minds of many modern Christians. *But* when we have thought all this, felt all this, said all this, we come back to the central question: When I pray is Anyone there? Do the words that are my spirit and my personal life reach the spirit and the life of a personal God? For me the matter is settled by the word of Christ: "This is how you should pray: Our Father . . ." And in spite of all times of skepticism and moments of doubt, when I consult my own soul I know that he is right. The Father is there. Our words may falter, our formulas may go dead; but the eternal God is unchanging and alive.

If we concentrate our attention on what is called "God-talk"—that is, the statements we make about God, we shall never find that renewal of the church, that revival of practical faith for which many on every side of the argument are seeking. Such real renewal comes not with talking *about* God but *to* him. Faith comes alive in the second person singular, not the third; with words that address, not words that describe. The latent atheism of our hearts can be fostered by endless discussion about God; it cannot survive the encounter of true prayer.

But what is it we say? Who is this God to whom I speak? There must be some conception in my mind, however dim, however inadequate, or I cannot really talk, cannot really hear. Isn't this our real problem? How can we pray unless we know at least something of God's reality and presence? We can be persuaded that meditation is good for us, that repeating holy words and having heartful thoughts does us good and helps to swing our world into better ways. But, in our hearts, we know that really to pray means talking to Someone; really to pray requires the conviction of God's

20

presence and response. So the Lord's answer to the "how" of prayer is "Say: Our Father in heaven."

"Our." Right away, if we are listening to what he says, we are delivered from one misunderstanding. Prayer—the most intimate, personal thing we do—is not directed to any private God. Even when we have gone to the little room and shut the door so that no one else can intrude, and "the busy world is hushed," it is still "our" Father to whom we speak—the God of the whole human family. If in our prayers we should begin to think about some antagonist—a personal opponent or an enemy of our nation—it is still "our" Father to whom we pray, and "our" includes every enemy. In this sense I would rather still think of God as "out there" than confine him to some ultimate in the depth of my own being. For "out there" he remains "our Father"—the Father of all men everywhere—and I know that, however personal my prayer, I do not come to him alone.

"Father in heaven." To me there is no way to reconcile these words with any purely "secular" reinterpretation of the faith. "Heaven" or "the heavens"—the word is there, however you like to interpret it. Jesus never defined heaven except to assert in this prayer that it is where God's will is done. We don't have to think of a place "up there," "out there," or even any place at all. If you don't like the word "supernatural" you don't

21

have to use it. But that there is a sphere, a realm, an order of life beyond the secular world that is, in some sense of the word, "the abode of God" is the clear belief of Jesus Christ, his apostles, and the saints of all ages. Of the relation of this realm to our secular life on earth the prayer has more to say. At this moment we simply pause to hear again the power of this simple phrase: "Our Father in heaven," to know that when we sincerely say these words, we are in touch with a world invisible that is the basis and the background of this world we see around us.

The God whom we seek in this vaster world, this eternal empire, this realm of mystery and the ultimate, we are to call "Father." That is the burning center of our Christian faith. It is no simple step to take—to call into the heart of the mystery, unto the Lord of all lords, the Creator of all that is, and use this familiar word: Father. It is the cry of faith, never to be taken for granted. It is not easy for modern man. It was not easy for our Christian ancestors when they saw the triumph of the pagan empires of their day. It was not easy for Stephen, the first Christian martyr, when he sank under the hail of stones, crying: "Lord, lay not this sin to their charge." It was not easy for the one who said: "My God, why hast thou forsaken me?" to say in the end: "Father, into thy hands I commit my spirit."

22

This is how to pray: into the unknown we send our voice: through the darkness we cry: in the teeth of skepticism and unbelief—our own or that of others—we say it: *Father.* It's a symbol, of course. Taken by itself it can conjure up very different pictures, for children know many different kinds of fathers on earth. But we do not take it by itself. Every portion of this prayer is not only spoken by Jesus Christ but soaked in his Spirit. The Father is his Father. If we want to know more nearly who he is, we think of the Son. When one of his disciples asked for a description of this Father of whom he so continually spoke, the reply came: "Have I been all this time with you, Philip, and you still do not know me? Anyone who has seen me has seen the Father." This is the God to whom we pray. What he is in himself we cannot know. What he is for the vast universe outside our ken we cannot even guess. But for us he is what Christ is—in goodness, compassion, justice, purity, and love. This is the Father we address in prayer—and this is why we often add "through Jesus Christ our Lord."

2. Room for Reverence

Hallowed be thy name.

If we pray at all, and if we use words when we do,
what *is* the first thing we are likely to say? I suggest
it will be some variant of the word "give." For,
etymologically, to "pray" is to ask; a prayer is a
request. So we start off by asking. "Give me
strength; give me wisdom; give me guidance; give
my family health; give help to those in trouble;
give to us peace in our time, O Lord." This is
the first thing that prayer means for most of us. If
it is not a means of getting something from God,
then we don't know what it is. I pray because I
am conscious of a lack, a need in myself, in other
people, and in our world; and I believe that God
can supply that need in his own way and in his
own time. So I am apt to go into that little room,
shut the door, and say to the Father in heaven:

24

"Give." For the millions today who still pray, although they have given up any habits of worship and are not at all sure what kind of God there may be, this is all there is to it. "Whoever you are—up there, out there, or in there—give."

At this point the skeptic says: "This is just what your religion is. You play it from weakness. You're just not prepared to accept the trials that come your way without calling for help. You're not willing to start cleaning up the mess the world is in, so you send out an SOS to the heavenly powers. You simply must have an omnipotent Father to lean on, so the churches have provided one for you. What you get is not an answer to your prayers, but a relief for your neurosis." We may protest right away that the great men of prayer have been, in fact, great men of action—from Jesus himself right on through St. Francis, and Luther, and Calvin, and Wesley, to Schweitzer and Dag Hammarskjöld—and we may ask politely if there is not such a thing as a neurotic rejection of the faith of our fathers. Yet nearly every one of us has at times wondered about this business of asking. "Give, give, give," we go on saying, but so often we don't seem to see any results. More than one person has told me that they have given up praying simply because, as they put it, "It didn't work."

If you expect me to say now that this kind of prayer is wrong, that we shouldn't ask for or expect

an answer, that praying is a kind of mystical meditation or an encounter in depth with our fellowmen, then you are wrong. I believe that we should
ask God to give. I believe we should go on asking
even when we don't understand the answers—
which like earthly fathers' answers can be "Yes" or
"No" or "Wait." And one powerful reason why
I so believe is that when Jesus Christ said, "This
is how you should pray," he included the petition,
"Give us this day our daily bread." That is a
sentence we shall be thinking about later in this
book. Meanwhile, I would draw your attention to
a point that is often missed—something that pro-
vides an answer both to the skeptic and to the
puzzled believer. Whereas with us "give" is normally the first clause in our prayers, in this model
prayer it is No. 4. Before we ever reach the point
of saying "give," we are to say: "Hallowed be thy
name. Thy kingdom come. Thy will be done in
earth as it is in heaven." If we are truly to take
this model as a guide and inspiration, then this
should set us thinking hard about the mood and
method of our prayers.

We are apt to begin by thinking about ourselves.
That's what the skeptic says we are doing all the
time—and too often he is right. Jesus says we
should start by thinking about God. Before we
ever come to the point of asking, we have to pause
to think about the One to whom we are talking.

But it's even more than that, more than just thinking about him. It's realizing his presence. It's letting ourselves be surrounded and gripped by the
holiness of God. This is where true prayer begins.
That is why the skeptic will never understand it,
for he has eliminated the dimension of the holy
and blocked the access of the Spirit. Prayer is not
something that can be wholly analyzed in rational
terms. It belongs to that deeper level of our being
where the body, mind, and spirit are fused and
we are open to the light that shines from the
Center, the presence and purpose of the living
God. The reason why those of us who try to pray
are often disappointed lies also here. We have, as
it were, rushed to God with our requests as if they
were all that mattered, treating him almost like a
machine for answering prayer. And so, quite naturally, we have often to confess that the machine
doesn't work. Our Lord does not tell us that we
mustn't ask. "Give" is a perfectly legitimate prayer.
What he does tell us is that we are inclined to
neglect the true atmosphere of prayer. We cannot
truly ask unless we have the spirit of reverence and
awe in the presence of our God and some sense of
the glory and mystery of his being. We are not
operating a machine, but talking to a Person. This
is how you should pray: "Our Father which art
in heaven, Hallowed be thy name."

I suspect that often these are the most meaning-

less words for us in the entire prayer. "Hallowing
the name" was an expression that was readily
understood by the Jews who first heard this prayer,
but neither the word "hallow" nor this idea of
the "name" is familiar to the average man today. In
the proposed Presbyterian *Book of Common Worship*,
in a service designed in contemporary speech,
the Lord's Prayer opens like this: "Our Father in
heaven, may your name be honored." That, perhaps, could be understood. Yet I wonder if at
this point in our prayer we really must fully understand. What we are doing is to realize the in-
expressible, to make room for that which can never
be explained in words. So perhaps it is better,
with most modern versions, to retain the word
"hallowed." For the original contains the word
"holy"—and this is one of these Bible words that
can never be translated into something else. Nor
can it be analyzed, for it speaks of that which
transcends the limits of our minds. It is, above all
others, the word that speaks of God himself.

This does not mean that when we say, "Hallowed be thy name," we are just muttering sounds,
a familiar mumbo jumbo that makes no sense.
There are words that have clear reference to things
we see and know—like table, pulpit, black, white,
big, little. There are others that point to that
which lies ultimately beyond our experience, but
which we can recognize in some small measure.

28

Such pointer words are beauty, truth, perfection, love. And the greatest of these is *holy*, which points to the very being of God himself—the source and perfection of the highest that we know. So when we begin to pray by saying, "Hallowed be thy name," we are letting the holiness, the wonder, the glory, the perfection of God himself invade our spirits and possess our minds. We are, as it were, detaching what we do from the mechanics of every-day, and creating the atmosphere of prayer. We do not then rush to our requests as though prayer was like picking up a telephone. We first realize the holy. We make room for reverence.

We are living at a time when reverence, the sense of the holy, the realization of the presence of God, is made more difficult than it was for many in the past. The farmer plowing his field, the fisherman spending nights on the open sea, the explorer battling his way through the jungle, were more apt to sense the mystery and know their dependence upon God than the clerk at the I.B.M. machine, the mechanic on the production line, or the astronaut with his eye on the delicate instruments of his craft. The advance of medical science, the increasing complexity of our industrial society, the pressures of a technological era, our detachment from the primary sources of our food and comforts—all these tend to breed a forgetfulness of the mystery that lies behind the glittering

civilization in which we live. So some are saying
that reverence, and a sense of God, are doomed
to vanish from the earth, and the day must come
when there will be no one in a world that man con-
trols to bow his head and say: "Our Father which
art in heaven, Hallowed be thy name."

Have you ever stopped to think what that
would really mean? It would not just mean that
worship would have ceased and all prayer be ex-
tinct. It would mean that we should live entirely
by the light of cold reason and mechanical efficiency. A newborn child would arouse no sense of
wonder, no twinge of mystery and awe. It would
simply be an event to be recorded, and eventually
regulated—perhaps according to the test-tube
methods of Huxley's *Brave New World*. The
death of a dear friend would give no cause for
reverence or holy grief. Indeed, if all this had
gone, we could scarcely call him "dear" at all. He
would be another unit of humanity, to be written
off the record when his day was done. The most
exquisite moment of delight in hearing great
music, or the rapture of poetry, would be analyzed
into some formula of psychology and explained
out of existence. Falling in love would be no more
than a chemical reaction. A world without reverence could be technically brilliant and coldly effi-
cient; but it would be a world in which no one

who knows what it is to be a human being would want to live.

Thank God, in spite of the trend toward a society in which nothing reminds us of the holy, in spite of the claims being made that we must learn to live in a merely secular dimension, nearly everybody still has at least some inkling of what it means to be in the presence of mystery that cannot be explained away, and experience of some moments when the only thing to say is: "Hallowed be thy name."

When President Kennedy was assassinated, did the nation shrug its shoulders and say: "Well, we know what happened. A shot was fired and a man was killed. That's all there is to it. Back to business." We know very well what happened. You cannot analyze it in precise words, but there was across the whole nation a sense of awe and reverence, something much more than mere sorrow and inevitable shock. There was a sense in which this was a hallowed moment for the nation and the world.

Not long ago I entered an elevator in a Washington hotel. The last person to follow me was an Air Force officer covered in ribbons. A lady in the car said, jokingly, "Press button 5 please; we might as well have some service from the Services." Someone else said: "Come from far?" The officer replied: "From Vietnam." Then the door opened

31

at his floor, and as he left us he said quietly: "I came home to bury my eighteen-year-old son." The doors closed and there was a silence in that car. I could say a holy silence, for there are moments in the rush of everyday life when we touch on that which cannot be expressed without a sense of reverence and awe.

But the sense of reverence is stirred in us not only by the unexpected and the tragic. Have you never stood before a vast spectacle of nature like the Grand Canyon and wanted to say: "Hallowed be thy name"? Would you not even in the very midst of the most joyful celebration, or the happiest of moments, want to say: "Hallowed be thy name"? Is there not at the peak moments of your life, whether in joy or sorrow, a sense of touching that which is beyond all words, so that the most fitting response is to use the words that can do no more than point to the ultimate, recognize the mystery, express the feeling of reverence and awe: "Our Father which art in heaven, Hallowed be thy name"?

How should we pray? Begin like this, says our Lord—and surely he knew our deepest need. We think it is for the gifts that God can provide. He knows it is for God himself—a communion with the Lord who made us. Begin here, he says. Make room for reverence first. Open your whole self to the God who seeks you and hallow first his name.

He is the source of these feelings of reverence. He is the one whom we must know as truly as we can before we can enter into that friendship in which we bring him our requests. If we learned more deeply to hallow his name, we should begin to see more amazing answers to our prayers.

In what practical ways can we make more room for this reverence in our lives? Surely by starting each day with the hallowing of his name. We may all do this in different ways, but it means that we do not rush out into the traffic of our affairs without the pause that remembers God. What better way to make that pause than just to use these words: "Hallowed be thy name"? They link us across the centuries with all our Christian ancestors, and with the thoughts and words of Jesus Christ himself. They bring before us the immensity of the love of God, the glory of the world that he has made, and the bright value of every human soul that we shall meet.

Then, what else do we come to church for if not to make room in our busy schedule for a time when together we have no greater purpose than to hallow the name of God? All our worship is designed for this, above all other ends. And there is no more reverent moment in the whole of our activities from week to week and month to month than when we bring into the sanctuary the symbols of our material life and make them the glowing reminders of the holiest moment in our human story. For the most hallowed event the world has known is the death and resurrection of Jesus Christ our Lord. And the most hallowed experience that is open to us all is when in simple faith we partake of the bread and wine. This is *holy* Communion. When in the silence we meet with our Lord, we shall understand why, before all else in the prayers that we make, he taught us to say: "Our Father which art in heaven, Hallowed be thy name."

3. Toward Heaven on Earth

Thy kingdom come.
  Thy will be done in earth, as it is in heaven.

In the city of Edinburgh there is a football team
that rejoices in the name "the Heart of Midlo-
thian" and is popularly known as "the Hearts." It
is a team that arouses intense local loyalty along
with a spirit of lively criticism not unknown among
the followers of baseball in the United States. In
fact, you might say that its supporters live in a state
of constant dissatisfaction with its performances,
and you can start an animated conversation at
almost any time and any place in Edinburgh
with the simple question: "What's wrong with
the Hearts?" It is as though the population had
a vision of football perfection before their eyes,
in the light of which their favorites are seen to
leave room for improvement.

35

The same question arises, of course, in much more serious matters. In recent years I'm sure you've heard people ask: "What's wrong with New York?" expressing their conviction that the city is either not what it was, or what it could be. Others, facing the disquieting signs of increasing crime, moral confusion, strikes, riots, or what seems to be easy affluence and lack of initiative, ask: "What's wrong with the nation?" And nearly every month a book is published whose subtitle could be: "What's wrong with the churches?" (It's one of the easiest books to write, and even if it contains no positive suggestions, someone is sure to call it "bold," "provocative," and "revolutionary.") Every day of our lives we read the columnists and listen to the commentators whose major theme is: "What's wrong with the world?" And, on top of it all, we have the avalanche of books, lectures, and sermons by psychiatrists and the clergy whose sole topic is: "What's wrong with you and me?"

It may well be that at the moment this question is being asked overmuch, but it is really extraordinary that we ask it at all. Why should human beings come to the conclusion that there is something wrong? Why not accept things as they are, as apparently the animals do? There is no evidence that monkeys are worried about the state of the simian world, or that in an African swamp the question is being raised: "What's wrong with the hippopotamuses?" Yet man no sooner appears anywhere on earth than he begins to look around and find that conditions could be improved. In less time than we guess, someone will be up there raising the question: "What's wrong with the moon?"

I suggest that behind this constant question there lies a vision of perfection like that which the supporters for the Hearts nourish for their favorite football team. For some strange reason, it seems, the human race is haunted by the dream of a much better state of affairs than we at present enjoy. This has always been understood by the great religions of the world, by the great artists, by the most profound philosophers, and by the enlightened statesmen. They have accepted the fact that we are restless because there is something much better to be realized than we have yet found. In their own several ways they have expressed what we often sing in the old Hebrew hymn, "Thou hast eternal life implanted in the soul." They can ask what is wrong because deep down they have a vision of what is right; and they rejoice in the continual quest for what is better.

There are some today who would have us stop asking this question. "There's no use asking what's wrong," they say, "because nothing whatever can be done about it. Things are as they are, and we had better accept them." In some quarters a pragmatic philosophy is gaining ground which would fit man into the natural and animal world without remainder. All our dreams, our visions, our hopes for something better are simply mirages that cannot affect the brute fact that nature will take her course. Therefore we need not worry ourselves about what seems wrong. It just is—and the next step will come along in the course of evolution. We have no more control over our destinies or valid hopes for the future than does the monkey or the hippopotamus. In popular terms this philosophy is expressed every day by those who tell us that "there will always be wars, always be slums, always be gangsters, always be corruption" and reject all the impulses of idealism. They are apt to say, "It's just human nature"—which is only a half-truth. It is human nature to ask what is wrong, to seek what is better. Merely to accept what is, is vegetable nature, animal nature.

Others go on asking the question: "What's wrong?" but they are inspired by no vision of what a full, rich, and happy human community could be. They are simply concerned with efficiency. They see humanity as a huge complex machine, and when they ask: "What's wrong?" they indicate that there are some mechanical defects that need to be put right. For them society is like an automobile that is not functioning efficiently, and their remedies are overhaul, adjustment, tuning-up, and better maintenance. They never raise the question of what the car is really for, or where it should be going. They simply want it to function more smoothly. So their answer to the sickness of mankind is usually along the lines of: "There's nothing wrong with the world that a little more education, a little more technology, a little understanding of the social machinery will not put right."

Everybody knows that there is a Christian point of view about this gap between what we are and what we might be. In fact, it often seems as though the major effort of the church is directed to telling everybody what's wrong. Sermon after sermon, book after book, seems to have one subject: What's wrong with the nation? what's wrong with the world? what's wrong with you and—of course— what's wrong with the church? The answer given is, what in the past was simply known as "sin," although today you are more likely to hear of alienation, frustration, meaninglessness, and ego-centricity. Whatever you call it, the diagnosis the Bible offers is relatively simple. We are shown that mankind is meant to live in a harmony of God's design. When his rule is acknowledged, when his will is done, then each human being reaches true fulfillment, and society develops in peace and understanding toward a richer and fuller life for everyone. What's wrong with us, then, is that both as individuals and as groups we tend to reject

39

the rule of God and seek some other lord, and to substitute for his will our own selfish desires.

The objection to this view is usually that it seems to suggest that we must lose our freedom and become the mere puppets of a heavenly King. But the point of the biblical picture is that God will not impose his rule and his will upon us. He leaves us free; and the discovery that we are left to make is that we are actually more free, more truly human, when we willingly submit to the rule of God and conform to his will. A simple illustration is that of the symphony orchestra. Is an individual violinist more free when he decides to ignore the conductor and go his own way, or when, in the accepted discipline of music, he is caught up in the orchestral unity within which he himself finds a more perfect self-expression? When the Christian says that what's wrong with the world is our rebellion against the rule of God and our resistance to his will, he is expressing the belief that there is a God to whom the whole world owes allegiance, that "in his service there is perfect freedom," and that when he is rejected, other powers—human and demonic—will inevitably disrupt society by seeking to be gods.

One way or another, that is what the church is saying in answer to the question: "What's wrong?" But the sad thing is that often we appear to have little else to say. We are too often the analysts of evil, the diagnosticians of disaster. It's time we remembered that we are first of all commissioned to announce good news. It is a *gospel* we have been given and there is no gospel in telling people what is wrong. The major question, after all, is not "What's wrong?" but "What can we do to put it right?" And the gospel answers that question on the basis of what *God* has done to put it right.

When Jesus taught us to pray, "Thy kingdom come: Thy will be done," you will notice that he assumed there was something wrong. You don't pray for something that is already happening. You don't find our Lord indulging in any analysis of evil. He saw it round him. He saw men and women who obviously had rejected God's rule in favor of their own. He knew the arrogance, the cruelty, the pride in the human exercise of power. He saw every day the suffering, the illness, the greed, the hostility that were to him quite contrary to the will of God. (Anyone who thinks that the prayer: "Thy will be done" means resignation in face of disease, accident, and death has never watched Jesus in action against these things in the name of his heavenly Father's will.) What he was concerned with was not diagnosis but cure.

What was it? Read his recorded words and you will see that two major themes dominated all he said—the kingdom of God and the will of God, God's rule and God's will. And these were not for him mere distant visions. He did not hold out the vision of the kingdom as a mirage gleaming on the distant horizon. He announced it as a present possibility. His first proclamation, according to Mark, was: "The time is fulfilled, and the kingdom of God is at hand: repent ye and believe the gospel." The rule of God is here, he said, the Kingdom is in your midst. And he didn't talk of the will of God as some kind of eternal law by which everything automatically happened, a predetermined divine party line to which all are forced, willy-nilly, to conform. He spoke of it as a living presence, a power for good, for health, for fulfillment that is pressing in on us for acceptance. At any moment this will of God can be released into the sickness of the world, the confusion of our hearts. It is in this mood that he prayed, and taught us to pray: "Thy kingdom come. Thy will be done in earth as it is in heaven."

For him the rule of God and the will of God are not distant ideals but a present hope, the great deliverance offered to men who know that there's something wrong. God's help, God's grace, God's guidance, God's recreative power are not just, as it were, laid up in heaven. They are right here —and our contact with them is prayer. For prayer is, first and foremost, not seeking to impose our will on God, but seeking to get our wills in line with his. How often we take our passionate desires to God and ask him to make things turn out the way we want them; how seldom we really expose ourselves to the risk of knowing his will and thus finding the backing of his rule.

Before we think further about his exciting way of prayer, let me remind you again of the One who is teaching us. If we are inclined to set aside this thought of the reality of God's rule and God's will being done on earth as it is in heaven, we need to remember that it has been done. Right here on this earth, in a time of much misery and unrest, there was a Man who was entirely submitted to the rule of God and constantly in touch with his will. And no one can say that this made the life of Jesus that of a mere puppet in the hands of a heavenly Father. It was from his perfect submission to the rule, his constant contact with the will of God, that he derived that amazing freedom that has astonished the world. This is why we can say that in him the kingdom came. He was the embodiment of God's rule on earth. He was the will of God translated into the flesh and blood of our human life. When *he* prayed: "Thy kingdom come: Thy will be done," the answer was already there.

But what about us? Do we still believe that the life we know on this earth—our own baffled and mixed-up lives, the fearful confusions, dangers, diseases, and hostilities of the world around us

43

—can in any way be moved toward the perfection of God's design? Is there really any possibility of edging this earth nearer heaven? Can you and I be better people? Can our church, our city, our nation, our generation around the world be moved closer to the kingdom? If we don't really think this possible, we had better give up this prayer. For it is a mockery to pray, "Thy kingdom come: Thy will be done," if we don't believe that either God's rule or God's will can have any practical effect on us or the society we live in.

Our Lord asks us to believe that the kingdom and the will of God are the greatest realities with which we have to do, and the ultimate factors in the destiny of men. So he teaches that our first duty after hallowing the name of God is to hold up before him every detail of our daily life, every concern we have about what's wrong in the city, the church, the nation, and the world, and say: "Thy kingdom come: Thy will be done." If all of us did it; if all of us meant it; if all of us were thus open to the inrushing of the powers of the kingdom, the refreshment of God's active will, who can tell what amazing changes would happen before our very eyes?

As I tried to enter into the meaning of these familiar words, it struck me that one reason why they often fall from our lips so formally and dead is that we are the victims of horizontal thinking.

44

What I mean by that is that we tend to have a mental picture of our journey through life, and that of all mankind, as leading along a horizontal plane. At one end, as it were, is the will of God. He has planned, right back in the beginning, all that is going to happen to us. At the other end is the kingdom of heaven, whether we think of it as our arrival at the goal of life eternal or the final consummation of the human story in the perfect society of God. It is true that there is a journey for us, and for humanity. It is true that there are goals to be reached. But when we think only horizontally like this, then we get distorted images of what is meant by the kingdom and the will of God. His will seems something fixed and cold, and his kingdom a very distant mirage. So our prayer loses all reality and power.

But suppose we think vertically. To me this is what our Lord is so often saying. The kingdom will have its fulfillment: yes, but now, right now, it is breaking in. God's rule is seen where self-will is broken, where peace is restored, where new hope is given to the poor and the hungry, where love replaces hate, and beauty ugliness. The man or woman who lives in the kingdom knows heaven here on earth. The will of God is indeed the final authority in all the world, but in the thought of Jesus it is not a decree but a living presence. As God is alive, so is his will. It meets us now, vertically, and is to be discovered by us day by day, moment by moment. The line in the hymn, "Thy joy to do the Father's will," doesn't suggest looking up an ancient, dog-eared timetable to see what has been decreed, but surely a lively contact with what God wants now. Why do we think of the will of God as away back in the past, at the beginning of time, and the kingdom of God as a faintly glimmering ideal far away in the future? To think vertically is to realize that both the rule and the will are here and now—as they obviously were for Jesus Christ.

"In earth, as it is in heaven." This is the purpose of the prayer—that this world where we keep asking "What's wrong?" may be penetrated now by the rule and the will of God, which are the content of heaven. It's not "a happy land, far, far away," but the dimension of God that surrounds us now. And when we pray this prayer the channels are opened for heaven to come in. "Thy kingdom come: Thy will be done"—beginning in me.

4. Why Ask for Bread?

Give us this day our daily bread.

What sense does it make for a company of well-fed, intelligent, modern Americans to bow their heads in church and say together: "Give us this day our bread"? Are these words ritual or real?

We all know the difference. When I meet you in the street and say, "How do you do?" these are ritual words. They are not much more than a friendly noise which we exchange without even waiting for an answer. But if you were desperately ill and I came to the hospital and asked the nurse at the door: "How is he doing?" these would be real words, and I should wait anxiously for the answer. Would any stranger dropping into our services in the middle of the Lord's Prayer, knowing nothing about Christian worship, and hearing us murmuring, "Give us this day our daily bread," think we were using real words or would it just sound like ritual? (The mere fact that we murmur makes it sound like ritual. When I was a small boy and heard passages read from the Bible about the terrible things that happened to the Israelites because they "murmured," I linked it up with the way we said our prayers!)

Of course, whenever we use the same words regularly, that's a ritual. There can be no public worship without some form of ritual. But the secret of true worship is letting the ritual become more and more real. And one of the reasons why we are studying the Lord's Prayer is that the ritual of this repeated prayer may begin to glow with life and meaning. There's a way of saying the Lord's Prayer which is no more than a passing "How do you do?" to God. There's another way in which each phrase becomes a real prayer, and we are truly awaiting a response. Let me ask: How serious are you when you ask God for daily bread?

We had better face the fact right away that we are not living in the same conditions as the people to whom Jesus first taught these words. Our surroundings are different; our wants are different; our understanding of the world is different; our expectations are different; our training is different; our thinking about religion is different. It's as though a series of curtains had come down between us and a prayer like this, so that very easily

it can cease to be real and become mere ritual.
In ancient days out in the prairie a wild dog
would turn around several times to see if any
danger threatened before settling down for the
night. Today the poodle in his comfortable city
apartment will probably go through the same mo-
tions; they are no longer real, just a ritual. I have a
feeling that we often say such "poodle prayers"
—more an unconscious tribute to our ancestors
than a real conversation with God.

One of the curtains that we have to pierce if
this particular prayer is to become real to us is
that of our modern technical civilization. We must
be aware of the totally different environment in
which we now live, and that the assumptions in
our minds are quite other from those of the men
and women who sat on the hillside in Galilee long
ago. We are not Palestinean peasants, tilling our
own strip of ground and waiting anxiously each
year for the harvest on which our life would literally depend. Bread for us is always in supply just
around the corner, and for many it is no more than
an extra which the diet-conscious nobly try to do
without. We have about as much difficulty in
imagining an urgent need for a loaf or a roll as did
Marie Antoinette, who, when she was told that
the mob was clamoring for bread, replied: "Let
them eat cakes." We live on the cakes of our
affluent society. We assume that the materials for

the complicated meals we eat will be there so long as we have money to buy them. So for modern man a basic prayer would more honestly be for dollars than for bread.

But surely that makes us think. You can't eat dollar bills. They are the symbol of a most intricate economy by which we obtain the food we need. Modern civilization is a fantastic achievement of the human spirit, but it is a delicate organism more easily subject to disruption than we allow ourselves to think. While for us it may be a thick curtain hiding from us the reality of a prayer for bread, it is in fact so thin that a sudden rent would soon reveal to us that the basic needs of man have not changed in five thousand years. If a city like New York were cut off from its sources of supply, within a few days people would be clamoring for bread. Yes: actually *bread*, for although a hungry man will lust for succulent banquets, a starving man thinks of little else but bread. You and I are, in the end, not so differently made from the peasants of Galilee. Our bodies need food, and the grain that is baked into bread has been shown to contain the vital ingredients for sustaining life.

One evening in Normandy in the summer of 1940, I sat down to an exquisite meal in a fine restaurant prepared with all the skill of French cuisine. Ten days later, as a prisoner of war, I was literally begging for bread. It can happen as quick-

50

ly as that. And when in our first camp the ration for the next day was issued every evening—one loaf to be divided among eight men—the words, "Give us this day our daily bread," took on a new meaning. It was not just that I remembered my New Testament Greek and knew that the word translated "daily" almost certainly means "for to-morrow," and so felt near to those early Christians who prayed this prayer in the evening with their thoughts on the next day's supply. It was the relevance of the prayer itself. If I were to ask God for anything at all at that time, my first thought would be bread. It was the immediate need for us all. Lofty thoughts about not considering material things and asking only for spiritual strength were, I confess, not in the picture. This was a need—a desperate, all-consuming, really humiliating need. Gone were the pious commentaries that insist that Jesus meant us to pray for spiritual bread. I knew what he was talking about, and understood why this came first. Of course he taught that we have still greater needs. We need God; and his prayer starts off with that—"Hallowed be thy name." We need the confidence in his rule and the fortifying of his will; and his prayer takes care of that—"Thy kingdom come: Thy will be done." But when it comes to our basic needs, he teaches us to pray first for daily bread. "Man shall not live by bread alone" was his word when he was tempted to sell

51

his soul by turning stones into bread; but no one really knows the power of that saying who has not first learned what it means to pray with an empty stomach: Give us bread.

But it surely is not necessary for all of us to go through an experience like this in order to realize how thin is the curtain of our modern civilization, how precarious the affluence we take for granted. We surely have the imagination to know that at this very moment millions—perhaps one third of all human beings on this earth—are right down there where bread is the gnawing, dominating clamor of the soul. Yes; I say "soul" deliberately, for basic hunger is not merely a matter of the body's demand. The desire for bread can fill the mind to the exclusion of almost all else, and the whole interior life of a man or woman can be a prey to it.

Have you noticed what the prayer is? "Give us this day our daily bread." Who is this "us"? Those of us here present? Our family? Our nation? In the mind of Jesus, "us" has one vast, inclusive meaning. It is the whole family of mankind. When you kneel, after a day in which your own bodily needs have been cared for—and how much more! —and say, "Give us each day our daily bread," your prayer not only reminds you of your plenty; it is for the feeding of that family, perhaps not so far away, where there are too many mouths for the food available; for that emaciated boy sleeping on the streets of Calcutta; for that woman up in the Andes who has nothing for her children to-morrow; for all whom Jesus teaches us to remember in this prayer. "Give us this day our daily bread!" —we are joining in the cry of the family to which we belong. And, as with every prayer that Jesus prompts, there must be action to follow. Could you sit down with a hungry man before a loaf of bread, say grace, and then eat the whole of it your-self? Even if it were your loaf, bought with your money? At this very hour Christians are praying: "Give us our daily bread."

With this understanding of our common hu-manity across time and space, we have penetrated the shining curtain of our technical, affluent society, and already the prayer for bread becomes more real. But there is still another curtain that hangs between us and this prayer. It is formed by our conception of religion and what true prayer can be. We have been taught to think of religion as the "spiritual" segment of our life. It is sup-posed to deal exclusively with the invisible values and eternal truths. The principle of separation of church and state, which originally had to do with the rejection of an established church with special privileges, has been extended in the popular mind to a separation of the sacred and the secular, of the spiritual and the material, of religion and the society where we earn our daily bread. Hence it is a shock to find this loaf of bread—this symbol of our basic physical need—right in the middle of a prayer to God. Again and again I have heard someone say: "I don't believe in praying for material things. I pray for courage, for faith, for spiritual strength." The implication is that this alone is mature prayer; only a child prays for *things*.

This is an acute difficulty for many people, and it makes this petition for daily bread a mere ritual expression of our general dependence upon God. We are thus removed from the men and women to whom Jesus spoke, whose faith at this point was quite simple and direct. When he said we should go into a "closet" for our prayers, the word he used was probably the word for "larder." The place where the food was stored would often be the only corner of a poor home where one could really be alone. We may imagine Jesus himself, as a young man in the home at Nazareth, slipping into the larder in the evening hour and with his eyes on the slender store of provisions for the coming day praying: "Give us each day our daily bread." For him and for those he later taught, there was no sharp distinction between the spiritual presence he sought as he hallowed the name of the heavenly Father and the material needs that were before his eyes. It was all God's world; and he talked to the Father as naturally about bread as about his heavenly kingdom.

Perhaps we have come to think that this kind of asking for material things implies a magical view of prayer. We feel superior to our distant ancestors because we know so much more about how the universe ticks, and therefore how bread is actually produced. They prayed to God for their daily food. We set the skills of modern science to work. Their answer to hunger was to cry to God. Our answer is a worldwide effort to raise the standard of living backed by the resources of the experts on nutrition. It looks as though, while we are mumbling in our churches: "Give us this day our daily bread," the real answer is being given by the researcher, the technician, and the statesman. We think the choice has now been made. While in the past man was helpless before the mysterious forces that caused the crops to grow and therefore called upon his God, now we know what's what and are on our way to mastering the food problem by human skills. So we don't need to pray for bread any more. We keep our prayers, if any, for those unseen gifts and graces that belong to the world of spirit.

Are we so sure that this is really the choice that confronts us now? Are we right in imagining that our Lord and his disciples were using this prayer as a means whereby a miracle could be worked and bread supplied without their effort? You will remember the first temptation recorded by Mat-

thew: "When he had fasted forty days and forty
nights, he was afterward an hungered. And when
the tempter came to him, he said, If thou be the
Son of God, command that these stones be made
bread." *That* was a prayer for miracle. And what
was the Lord's reply? "It is written, Man shall not
live by bread alone, but by every word that pro-
ceedeth out of the mouth of God." He com-
pletely rejected the temptation to use God as a
divine magician to solve a human problem. When
he prayed for bread he was fully aware of the net-
work of human forethought, skill, and labor that
would produce the loaf. He never separated the
human and the divine in such a way as to say:
"The sun and the rain and the capacity of growth
are God's business. He is not concerned with the
plowing and the sowing and the reaping and the
distribution—that is man's business." For him
there was no special section of life labeled "religion." Everything was God's, and his kingdom
encompassed the seed, the sparrow, the sower, the
miller, the housewife—and, he would add today,
the laboratory, the tractor, the silo, the technician,
and the politician.

If we are to believe in God today, it will not be
in a god of limited jurisdiction, a god who rules
over a steadily decreasing area of mystery while
man pushes his control farther and farther into
the recesses of nature. Nor can it be a god who is

only concerned with a section of life we isolate with the words "spirit" or "soul." Physical science, medical science, philosophy and theology today are more and more agreed that an absolute dichotomy between matter and spirit, soul and body, the sacred and the secular simply cannot be maintained. There is a unity in the universe, a unity in our experience of life—and for Christian faith it is a unity that finds its source and fulfillment in the creating and redeeming God. The God we believe in is Lord of all. So when we pray to him: "Give us this day our daily bread," we seek no miracle. We ask that he will work through every agency of his creation—the soil, the germ of wheat, the laborer, the scientist, the economic system—to sustain in life this whole human family. Our prayer is not an incantation, but a lifting of the human will to God, so that his will—which is for the welfare of us all—may increasingly be done. To pray this particular prayer in our day will surely include the thought that now at last it is possible so to increase the world's supply of food that no one need go hungry.

So we are led to the final curtain that makes this prayer unreal. We can see that even in our complex world our basic needs are the same as ever. We can see that this prayer is not a superstition which we have outgrown, but that it chimes in with our new understanding of the unity of the material and spiritual. But now we are face to face with the ultimate question: Do we believe this God is real, or is he an imaginary power? It comes to this in the end; for how can a prayer for bread be real if God himself is not real? "Pray like this," said Jesus: "Father in heaven, give us this day our daily bread." If the curtain of doubt and skepticism that hangs between us and this heavenly Father can be pierced, then no matter what questions still remain, this prayer will live.

Let me say this, quite bluntly. Once we have really heard who it is that Jesus Christ represents and calls on us to trust, it is no more easy and no more difficult to put our faith in him than it was at any period of human history. The choice is exactly the same. Either we human beings are, along with whatever intelligent beings there may be on the stars and planets unexplored, the only guiding and controlling power, solely responsible for the means of life and death, or else there is a God in charge of all that is, whose ways are ultimately beyond our understanding but who has revealed enough to give us cause to trust him, to love him, and to seek to do his will. Jesus Christ brings me such a God, and in his name I am ready to pray a real prayer with all who believe in simple words that are burning with meaning at this present hour: "Father in heaven, give us this day our daily bread."

5. Forgiveness—Passive and Active

And forgive us our debts,
  as we forgive our debtors.

If this prayer is to be a model for us in our conversation with God, we shouldn't miss the order in which each sentence comes. The prayer begins, not with us and our needs, but with God. We learn right away that it's not a psychological exercise we are engaged in, but an effort to meet with God. Of course we may meet him at every point in our daily life—in our work, in a conversation with a friend, at the dinner table, strap-hanging in the subway, or as we read the newspaper headlines. But prayer is the moment when we are doing nothing else but seeking God. So, says Jesus, begin by fixing your thoughts on him—"our Father in heaven"—and then take time for the wonder of his presence to possess you—"hallowed be thy name." You will then realize that nothing you have to say can possibly matter more than your acceptance of *his* rule and your discovery of *his* will. "Thy kingdom come: Thy will be done." Only then does this prayer turn to our immediate needs, the things we want God to do for us.

This is not to say that prayer must always be a formal and orderly business. If I were ejected from the cockpit of a plane and found myself plummeting to earth, I doubt if I should bother much about the correct approach to God before praying for that parachute to open. But if we are serious about learning to pray, and about knowing what Christ himself had to say about it, this order is important. The preliminary concentration upon God, his being, his rule, and his will, will gradually educate us, and we'll find that our requests and our expectations will begin to change. (You can hardly pray: "Thy will be done: make me rich and eliminate my competitors"; or, "Thy kingdom come: blast Hanoi and Peking to hell.")

When the prayer does turn to our requests, in what order do they come? What we learn here is exactly what Jesus Christ thinks about our deepest needs. And the answer is surprising. For the first request shocks us by its blunt materialism, and the second by its emphasis on something that we would rather forget. The first, to put it another way, disturbs the devout churchman who finds it most "unspiritual" to pray for daily bread; the second disturbs the man in the street who doesn't think forgiveness is all that important. Yet, according to the Lord himself, these are our two basic needs—and these are what we should pray for first. Give—and forgive. Give us bread: forgive us our sins—in that order. In the last chapter I spoke of the blunt prayer for bread, for us and the whole human family. How refreshing is the holy common sense of Jesus—for how can there be any sins to forgive unless first we are sustained in life?

The question now before us is forgiveness. Suppose we have swallowed our pride and accepted that the human race is still dependent upon God for physical survival. Let me ask: Do you honestly put this question for forgiveness on the same level as the prayer for bread? I am not asking a hypothetical, churchy question to which the standard reply would be: "Of course forgiveness is absolutely central to our faith and matters much more than material things like bread." I am asking if, at a critical moment when you desperately needed food to keep you alive, you would have anything like the same intense, consuming desire to be assured of the forgiveness of God? Have you ever prayed for forgiveness with the passion that drives a prayer for relief from pain or for the healing of one you love? In the mind of Christ, as we see from all his deeds and words, forgiveness, both

61

divine and human, is, like our daily bread, a
matter of life and death. To be forgiven is to be
right with God, right with our fellowmen; and
fullness of life belongs to those who "hunger and
thirst" for this rightness. The unforgiven are the
damned. In his eyes, forgiveness is to the soul
what bread is to the body. This is why he offers
to us in his Holy Communion the divine forgiveness in the form of bread.

"Pray like this: forgive us our debts." Let's
pause to straighten out this "debts" and "trespasses" business. In my church, a bunch of Presby-
terians acknowledge their debts, while, two blocks
away, our friends at St. James' are confessing their
trespasses. We mean, of course, exactly the same
thing; and I'm not prepared to admit that, while
Episcopalian ancestors in an English village knew
all about trespassing, our Scottish ancestors found
the financial metaphor much more congenial! We
use the prayer as it stands in the Gospel of Matthew. "Trespasses" occurs in the verses that follow
the prayer, and found its way into the Latin
version of the prayer, whence it reached the *Book
of Common Prayer*. Since both expressions are
metaphors—and neither conveys immediately to
modern man what is meant—the translators of
the New English Bible have boldly, and I think
wisely, given us this reading: "Forgive us the wrong

we have done, as we have forgiven those who have
wronged us."

"Forgive us the wrong we have done." This is
how we are to pray. The first two things we are to
ask of God is that he will keep us alive and pardon
our sins. Our natural life and health depend on
getting our daily bread; our spiritual life and
health depend on getting our sins forgiven. Our
Lord held these two necessities very close together.
For him the total health of people like you and
me consisted in release from bodily ills and depri-
vation and release from the guilt of our wrong-
doing. Thus he could say to a paralyzed man
lying on a stretcher—a man whom his friends so
desperately wanted to be cured that they had
broken into the roof of the house where Jesus was
and let him down to the floor in front of him—
"Your sins be forgiven you." Sometimes we hear it
said that Jesus Christ had a free and easy attitude
toward human failings and softened the stern
religious teachings of his day. It was the Pharisees
who were obsessed with sin and guilt, and, un-
fortunately, after the brief, bright interim of Jesus'
teaching, the whole miserable subject was resur-
rected and fastened round the neck of Christianity
by that ex-Pharisee Paul. This is not what I find
in the New Testament. Our Lord certainly turned
upside down ideas about sin and salvation (as
did Paul in following his Master). He smashed

through the current distinction between the sinner and the righteous. But, if you note what he said and what he did, you will find that he was not announcing that everyone was righteous, but that everyone—including, with the greatest emphasis, those who thought they were good—is a sinner. "Jesus saw the good in every man." Yes, this is true insofar as he knew what the very worst of humanity can become by the grace of God; but how about his description of that which lies inside us all? "From inside, out of a man's heart, come evil thoughts, acts of fornication, of theft, murder, adultery, ruthless greed, and malice; fraud, indecency, envy, slander, arrogance, and folly; these evil things all come from inside, and they defile the man."

Jesus Christ was an utter realist about these things—not a sentimentalist who believed that a little more goodwill all around would settle the troubles that afflict the human race. And, by and large, this generation agrees with him. The list of vices I have just read sounds almost like a syllabus of the modern novel, or a text to be hung over the Broadway theater. We know—and know much more clearly than our grandparents—that there's something wrong with us, a wrong that goes deeper than mere ignorance or maladjustment. The Christian therefore can share the agony of the artist and the insights of the sensitive psychiatrist and sociologist of today. But if he, and they, are listening to the word of Christ, the whole question of our guilt will be seen in another dimension. Its roots will be found in our rebellion against God. "Against thee, and thee only, have I sinned" is the cry ascribed to King David, who most certainly had appalling crimes against his fellowmen on his conscience. What the whole Bible, culminating in Christ, is thundering out is that there is a God whom we have wronged, and that every malady of the soul, every wickedness that stains our world, stems from our defiance of his will.

So Jesus says: Get this right first. Say: "Father in heaven, forgive us our sins." That's where the light breaks. That's where the difference lies between a sordid diagnosis of human evil, and the insight that leads to freedom. Leave God out, and there is nothing but endless analysis of our evils and our problems. If our wickedness is a dark, inscrutable shadow on a life that we know to be full of promise and endless hope, we can only grope for alleviation or wallow in despair. But if it is an offense against God, then God may forgive. The assurance of Christ is that God *will* forgive. "Forgive us our sins." The essence of the faith is not the grim recognition of our guilt, but the reality and certainty of pardon.

In a sense this is pardon in the passive tense. As we confess our sins in church the minister is

commissioned to declare our forgiveness in some
such words as these (from the new *Book of Common Worship*): "I declare unto you, in the name
of Jesus Christ, we are forgiven." It is passive, for
there is nothing we can do—except to receive, to
accept the good news. There is not one single
claim that we can make, not one down payment,
not one IOU. This is what the Bible calls grace,
and it is the glory of the Christian faith. We are
forgiven. To me the saddest thing about modern
atheism, in all its various shades, is not its claim
to produce the daily bread without God; we
know what that can mean. Nor is it its resolute
secularism; we can be secularists too. It is just the
ultimate fact that there is no one to forgive us our
sins. Our wrongs against one another can be con-
fessed and pardoned; but the ultimate wrong,
the deepest guilt, lies there untouched, and in a
silent universe there is no word of reconciling
power. This too is the emptiness of a theology
that has no personal God. Forgiveness, like love,
is personal—and the prayer that Jesus teaches is
directed to One who, however mysterious and beyond our loftiest thoughts, is "our Father."

Is this cry for forgiveness, this passive acceptance,
merely a selfish urge to clean our conscience and
be right with God? Note again the words that
Jesus used: "Forgive us our debts." This, too, is
a family prayer. Like the young Isaiah in the

Temple we don't only say: "I am a man of unclean lips"; we add, "and I dwell in the midst of a people of unclean lips," which was his way of expressing corporate guilt. In our services of worship, in our private prayers, we are called on to shoulder the guilt of others in order that God may lift it from us all. There is a magnificent prayer of Moses recorded in the book of Exodus: "Oh, this people have sinned a great sin, and have made them gods of gold. Yet now, if thou wilt forgive their sin—; and if not, blot me, I pray thee, out of thy book." Jeremiah, lying in the prison to which his preaching had brought him, agonizes for the people who had cast him there and brings an astonishing word of the Lord: "I will cleanse them from all their iniquity, whereby they have sinned against me." There is a ministry of intercession to which we are called in worship— even at the point where we confess our sins. There is a vicarious confession we are summoned to make, provided we remember that this is dangerous ground. We sing:

> O give us hearts to love like thee!
> Like thee, O Lord, to grieve
> Far more for others' sin than all
> The wrongs that we receive.

There is a kind of professional grieving for others' sins that is the opposite of Christian love. We are

67

called indeed to share in some remote degree the agony of Gethsemane, but not to parade in public our mourning for the sins of someone else.

If, then, this matter of God's forgiveness is so central, so vital, so urgent, why does this prayer not mean more to us? We have thought about the difference between the ritual and the real. Here again the distinction is obvious. If I bump into you mildly on the way out of a bus, I say: "I beg your pardon." That's ritual. We say it nearly every day—sometimes meaning no more than "Speak a little more loudly, can't you?" But if I had done you a serious injury, something that hurt badly and that weighed on my conscience, and I came to say: "I beg your pardon," that would be entirely different. It would be real. When we repeat in the Lord's Prayer, "Forgive us our debts," this is what we're saying to God. "I beg your pardon." Is it ritual or real? Again, our task today is to let what is inevitably ritual become more and more real. How?

The answer lies in the words that Jesus added to the request for pardon. They are immensely important. "Forgive us our debts, *as we forgive our debtors*"—"Forgive us the wrong we have done, *as we have forgiven those who have wronged us.*" The prayer for forgiveness becomes real and alive when we know what we are saying here.

In some ways this is the most unexpected part

68

of the whole prayer. What would have seemed normal to us, or to the Jews who first heard these words, would be something like this: "Forgive us our sins, because we are very sorry about them"; "Forgive us our sins, because we are truly penitent"; "Forgive us our sins, because we promise to try to be better." Not one of these thoughts is suggested here. The words he puts in our mouths are quite explicit: "as we have forgiven those who have wronged us." Notice, it's not "because." We're not claiming forgiveness because of what we have done about forgiving others. It's "as," which means that if, in all honesty we cannot say that we have forgiven others, we cannot ask for the forgiveness of God. If it is just not true that we have forgiven, then the first part of the prayer is a mere ritual and nothing happens. This is the plain and startling meaning of the words that Jesus taught.

He backed it up, you remember, with the story of the king and his servants. This was a matter of literal debts, and the parable is dramatic. The man who was pardoned his debt of ten thousand talents had no scruples in refusing the plea of his fellow servant to let him off his debt of a hundred pence. "Pay me what you owe." He would not forget; he would not forgive; he would not even wait. The enormous difference in the amounts owed is, of course, our Lord's way of telling us that the wrongs that people have done to us are infinitesimal compared with the wrong we have done to God. Do we believe that—in any practical sense? And the end of the story is terrible and unmistakable. The king heard what had happened and sent for the man. " 'You scoundrel!' he said to him; 'I remitted the whole of your debt when you appealed to me; were you not bound to show your fellow-servant the same pity as I showed to you?' And so angry was the master that he condemned the man to torture until he should pay the debt in full."

A rough story—and, of course, a parable, not an allegory in which we can make every detail speak. But the ending is by no means softened when Jesus adds: "And that is how my heavenly Father will deal with you, unless you each forgive your brother from your hearts."

If we think this is a dreadfully harsh way of speaking—so different from our casual way of assuming the forgiveness of God—then we haven't really considered the facts. I couldn't understand how Jesus could use this violent language about the unforgiving servant being tormented, until I began to think of the experience of men and nations as we know it. This is just how life works out. The person who refuses to forgive, who nurses a grudge, who indulges a permanent hate is, in plain fact, a tortured soul. As I was preparing this, I received a letter from a radio listener in another part of the country which expressed a terrible torment of spirit dating back to an incident, a hurtful experience, thirty years ago. There was still evident a deep resentment, a bitter—yet cherished—memory—and clearly there was no peace. So it is with a nation that cannot forgive. History is stained with the vendettas of tribes and states that nourish perpetual mutual hatred. There is only one way to break the vicious circle that tortures the human race—and that is the way of forgiveness. Once we have seen this we know why it was that our Lord put this in the forefront of our prayers: "Forgive us the wrong we have done, as we have forgiven those who have wronged us." The passive reception of the forgiveness of God only becomes real for those who are active in the forgiveness of their fellowmen.

This is perhaps the most searching point in the entire prayer—and the most potentially powerful. A Christian church should, among other things, be an oasis of forgiveness in the desert of our hates and fears. We can't go there to receive the forgiveness of God and then go out to exact retribution from those who offend us: "Pay what you owe me!" We are asked to lay there and leave there, in the oblivion of God's mercy, every hate, every resentment, every vengeful thought; and in utter

71

confidence to be assured of the complete forgiveness of God for all the wrongs we have done. Then we shall go out with the freedom of a clean conscience to be in our daily life the creative agents of forgiveness, the ambassadors of love.

6. Shelter or Rescue?

*And lead us not into temptation,
  but deliver us from evil.*

With these words Jesus closes his model prayer.
The doxology was added later by the church—
and Easter will tell us the reason why. It is with
these words that we rise from our knees and go out
to meet the world: "Lead us not into temptation,
but deliver us from evil." They are the bridge between the sanctuary where we have met with God
and the breakfast table, the subway, the office,
the daily round. We begin with the moment of
the purest adoration where we do nothing but
hallow the name of God, but we end with the din
and clatter of the city already ringing in our ears.
Our prayer has brought us from the holy of holies
through the completion of the kingdom and the
will of God to our requests for bread for our

bodies and pardon for our sins, and now sends us out into a world which is by no means the kingdom of heaven, a world where it is not at all easy to steer a Christian course through trials, temptations, dangers, minor irritations, and overwhelming evils. So the prayer that brings us to our feet—the open end of this moment of communion with our God—is: "Lead us not into temptation, but deliver us from evil." I could talk about "buckling on our armor," but let's be quite prosaic and say that this is the coat we put on as we pass through the door to meet what the day may bring.

"Lead us not into temptation." Here, for perhaps the first time in the sequence of this prayer, many want to call out: "Objection!" What's this we are being asked to say? "Father in heaven, *lead* us not into temptation." What kind of image is this to take with us into the daily round? If you are uncomfortable with this prayer, if—as some have told me—you just cannot use it all, I suspect the reason lies in the picture the words create in your mind. Here's God, who knows exactly what your weak points are, and he's preparing a series of traps for you, cunningly arranging for situations to arise where you are almost sure to fall into your besetting sins. If you lose your temper easily, he's planning to bring the most infuriating people across your path; if you are a glutton, he has prompted someone to offer you a most stupendous banquet; if you are inclined to drink to excess, he's going to have the stuff right under your nose; if you can't control your sex drives, he's got the most seductive situations all lined up for you; if you tend to gossip, he has already prepared some irresistible material; if you slip easily into little dishonesties, he's waiting with some subtle suggestions about these income tax returns. So we are to say: "Please, God don't do it: don't set these traps for me."

If that's your picture, it's better not to say the prayer. But I don't for a moment believe that our Lord had any such conception of his heavenly Father, or ever meant us to think of him as this kind of divine seducer. Perhaps the words as we have them are misleading. "Leading" does have a little bit of the suggestion of "enticing" or "entrapping," and "temptation" is a word we associate with an almost irresistible impulse, as when we say: "I was sorely tempted to tell him to go to hell." But we can get rid of any lingering notion of God setting traps for us and waiting to pounce when we fall by the quite explicit statement of one of Christ's apostles. James says: "Let no man say when he is tempted, I am tempted of God: for God cannot be tempted with evil, neither tempteth he any man." We can clear this picture right out of our conscious, or subconscious, minds.

What then can we mean when we say these

75

words? The New English Bible offers another translation: "Do not bring us to the test." We all know that there are experiences in life that are a test, or trial, for our Christian character. I am not thinking now so much of the kind of temptations to indulge our favorite sins as of the crippling blows that may strike us down at any time—a major disappointment, a dreadful accident, a sudden bereavement, or, in the wider world, a national catastrophe, an outbreak of war. It was toward such a test that Jesus moved when he rode into the city of Jerusalem on Palm Sunday morning. This was his trial that lay ahead—and he knew it. He knew also that, in another way, it was the supreme test for the people who cheered and shouted around that little procession, for the religious establishment that watched ominously from the city walls, for the military authorities who were on the alert that week in Jerusalem, for Pilate who would soon be confronted with a prisoner and his own conscience, and, in an excruciating way, for his own disciples. I don't think we can ever really understand what it means to pray: "Lead us not into temptation" until we have let the word grow into the dimensions of the Passion story, and have realized the immensity of the trial, the fearful testing, that comes when concentrated evil is let loose upon the soul.

I find that this phrase of the prayer requires

more insight, more spiritual imagination—and more humility—than perhaps any other. For it is easy to say: "All right, it's trials we are to think about rather than what we normally consider temptations; but isn't trial good for us? Ought we really to pray to be sheltered from everything that tempts our faith?" We tend to be ashamed of the element in our religion that implies shelter, security, refuge, safety. I confess that every time I decide to use a beautiful and familiar hymn a reluctance comes over me at asking people to sing:

> Jesus, lover of my soul,
> Let me to thy bosom fly,
> While the nearer waters roll,
> While the tempest still is high:
> Hide me, O my Savior, hide,
> Till the storm of life is past.

Do we really want to be tucked up securely like this, and rolled away in a religious blanket until the storm has died down? Is this the life to which Christ called his disciples when he asked them to take up the cross and follow him? Certainly, if there is a truth expressed in this beloved hymn, it needs to be balanced by the end of the service with a good rousing shout of, "Fight the good fight with all thy might," or "Soldiers of Christ, arise!"

But *is* there a truth behind this idea of shelter? If there isn't, then generations of Christians have been deluded by this hymn, and still more generations by the prayer to keep us from the test. We need to do some hard and humble thinking about our situation. As I have said before, this is a very realistic prayer. Our Lord, we are told, knows what is in man. He knows the stuff you and I are made of. He knows that testing and trial can be good for us. But he also knows that there are limits to our capacity to endure, dangers that can be too much for us at our present level of faith. So he teaches us to pray that we may be spared from them. "If you're going to be my disciple," he seems to say, "you'll have trials enough to test your faith. Don't go looking for more. There are dangers enough round the corner. Pray that you will be spared the one for which you are ill-prepared."

The truth is that, however much we should like to be the strong who can meet any test or trial, the invincible and resolute under all circumstances, we are in fact more frail and vulnerable than we know. You remember what our Lord said to Peter just before his arrest and trial? "I have prayed for thee, that thy faith fail not." And Peter was bold enough to answer: "Lord, I am ready to go with thee, both into prison, and to death." We know what happened before the cock's crow as the next

78

day broke. The man who wrote the old Lenten prayer said it for us all: "Almighty God, who seest that we have no power of ourselves to help ourselves; keep us both outwardly in our bodies and inwardly in our souls, that we may be defended from all adversities which may happen to the body, and from all evil thoughts which may assault and hurt the soul; through Jesus Christ our Lord." The power of evil is stronger than we know.

It is therefore not shrinking and weakness but sheer Christian common sense that makes us ask for both shelter and rescue as we face the hazards of this mortal life. If we have really taken the measure of the powers of evil, we confess our desperate need of the protection and deliverance of almighty God. There is nothing soft or superfluous about this final request to be kept from temptation and delivered from evil. It's the mark of a man or woman who has really taken up the challenge of evil. There is a military maxim: "Never underestimate the power of the enemy," and with that in mind we seek to be clothed in the armor of Christ. What we are telling the Lord as we cross the bridge that leads from the inner room to the traffic of the modern world is: "Keep me from the tests that might be too much for me; but if they come, then deliver me from the evil."

We need this prayer in a thousand situations

79

ranging from the comparatively trivial to the ultimate and terrible.

Suppose, for instance, that you have at times an irritable disposition and are apt to snap at people who annoy you—and feel miserable about it afterward. And let's say that you work in an office in close contact with several other employees. One of them gets on your nerves by making the same remark at the same time and in the same tone of voice every day. I could imagine you closing your prayers on some gloomy morning with the request: "Don't let him say it this morning: it would be too much for me—but if he does, then help me to keep my temper." That's it. "Lead me not into temptation, but deliver me from evil."

More seriously, suppose you are an alcoholic. I understand that it is one of the first principles of Alcoholics Anonymous that you admit your inability to control the craving by your own strength—which is exactly what Christ teaches us about our weakness in face of every kind of evil. Every day you know that situations will arise when temptation will rush in with overwhelming power. You have no self-assurance that you can cope no matter how severe the test. So there is no more real and heartfelt prayer than this: "Lord, don't let me get into that situation of terrible temptation—but if the test should come, then give your rescuing power." "Lead us not into temptation, but deliver us from evil."

Is there not some such prayer in the heart of every one of us as we contemplate the dangers and disasters to which we are all exposed? When we pause to think about it we know how terribly vulnerable we are, body and soul. We may pretend to be superior to our Christian ancestors who seemed almost obsessed by the risks and dangers that surround us. They prayed in the morning: "Grant that this day we fall into no sin, neither run into any kind of danger," and in the evening: "By thy great mercy defend us from all perils and dangers of this night." But we have simply drawn a gossamer curtain of sophistication over the mortal dangers that surround us still—the accident, the lethal germ, the maniac, the soul-devouring dictator, and the penultimate horror of a nuclear war. Is there then no meaning for us in the prayer that says: "Lord, shelter us; spare us from disaster—but if it should strike, come to our rescue." "Lead us not into temptation, but deliver us from evil."

What kind of deliverance do we think is possible in these extremities of life? According to the words and actions of Christ himself we must set no limits to the rescuing power of God. The inrushing powers of his kingdom are only held in check by our lack of faith. His good and perfect will for our total health of body and soul is only frustrated by the powers of evil. Christ calls for a greater confidence in the healing grace that the Father bestows upon his children. But he also speaks of the preservation of that inward self, that God-given self we call the soul. This is ultimately what matters, and since sooner or later the body must perish, he offers that inward deliverance that sustains and fortifies the soul. "What does a man gain," he once asked, "by winning the whole world at the cost of his true self?" It is that true self that he is able to deliver, no matter what catastrophes may fall.

This is why I spoke of a holocaust as the penultimate catastrophe from which we pray to be delivered. The ultimate catastrophe is the loss of the soul. Now we have reached the very center of this prayer, and it contains a truth so profound that we can only guess at the meaning it contained for him—especially on that day when he rode into the city where the powers of evil were massed for his destruction. "Do not bring us to the test," he taught his disciples to pray, "but save us from the evil one." What he was facing that day for us was the ultimate trial of the soul—the test that meant the unleashing of the full fury of the evil one.

As the cheering of the crowds echoed in his ears that morning he knew already that the die was cast. With tragic irony the orchestra of hell was playing a royal overture for the Son of man, who was delivered to the evil one. The trial of Jesus before Pilate was as nothing to the trial that was on between light and darkness, love and hate, hope and despair. Even the fearful torments that were to be inflicted on his body were as nothing to the agony of his descent to hell, the moment of utter darkness when meaning was drained out of life, when the evil one was triumphant, and he cried: "My God, my God, why hast thou forsaken me?" All that happened during Holy Week was the living out by Jesus of his own prayer. This was the final test when the skies of evil opened and the cosmic storm broke upon him with final fury. "Lead me not into temptation," "Do not bring me to the test"—was not that even his last prayer in the Garden of Gethsemane, a prayer that ended with the confident "nevertheless"—"nevertheless not as I will, but as thou wilt." For, even as this last test had to come, he knew that the Father was there to deliver him from evil.

Do you see now why he said to the disciples in the garden, "Watch and pray, that ye enter not into temptation"? It was this temptation he had in mind, the ultimate assault of the devil on the soul of man. And he knew that neither these disciples, nor you and I, are capable of withstanding such a storm. But—and this is the inner meaning of Holy Week—we need never pass in our

mortal weakness into this place where God seems
absent and the evil one is rampant. Our Lord has
been there for us. He rode into the valley of death
and desolation, not as a knight in shining armor,
but as the lowly, the innocent one, borne by a
donkey to an ignominious death. He was in solemn
truth led into temptation, brought to the final
test. And when the deed was done, and the skies
had cleared, he emerged the victor. He was delivered from evil. His disciples then knew, and
have known ever since, that the awful test is over,
that no one any more need descend into hell.
Thus we look back to the lonely figure who rode
into-Jerusalem and we know that indeed this is
the King of kings, the Lord of lords, for he is the
Deliverer from evil.

So the prayer, as our Lord has given it, comes
to an end. We rise from our knees each day to
meet the world as it comes, with the words, "Deliver us from evil," not as a faint and feeble hope,
but as the confident conviction of those who know
the victory is won. We can make our own the
words that Martin Luther wrote in another age
of change and stress and danger:

> Did we in our own strength confide,
> Our striving would be losing,
> Were not the right man on our side,

The man of God's own choosing:
Dost ask who that may be?
Christ Jesus, it is he;
Lord Sabaoth, his name,
From age to age the same,
And he must win the battle.

7. Defiant Doxology

For thine is the kingdom, and the power,
and the glory, for ever. Amen.

Since no one plunges into the last chapter of a
serial story without studying the synopsis of "what
has gone before," let me now offer you a complete
summary of the last six chapters. Here it comes:

> Our Father which art in heaven,
> Hallowed be thy name.
> Thy kingdom come.
> Thy will be done in earth,
> as it is in heaven.
> Give us this day our daily bread.
> And forgive us our debts,
> as we forgive our debtors.
> And lead us not into temptation,
> but deliver us from evil.

That's all. Now we're ready for the Easter text: "For thine is the kingdom, and the power, and the glory, for ever. Amen." That's the doxology, the hymn of praise, the roll of drums and the clash of cymbals with which the church closes the Prayer of prayers. And what else is being said or sung in a thousand languages wherever Christians meet on Easter morning? I call it the defiant doxology because it rises out of the Resurrection faith of the church in defiance of the world, the flesh, and the devil. In spite of the immense authority and terrible responsibility of the rulers of this world we still declare: "*Thine* is the kingdom"; in spite of the stupendous new powers that have been given to modern man, the man of flesh, secular man, we still confess: "*Thine* is the power"; in spite of the resplendent antics of demonic forces, the seductions of the current cults of magnificent despair, and the hypnotic fascination of the absurd and the abyss, we still raise the shout of adoration: "*Thine* is the glory." Easter means that in a world of jet diplomacy, intercontinental missiles, cybernetics, extrasensory perception, LSD, space probes, far-out cults, and everything-a-go-go, there are still men and women who can get up in the morning and say: "Glory be to the Father, and to the Son: and to the Holy Ghost; as it was in the beginning, *is now*, and ever shall be: world without end."

You may by now be feeling that I have not only given you a summary of all that has gone before, but have already supplied the beginning, the middle, and the end of an Easter sermon—so what is left but the Amen? But there is something I want to say about this doxology, about the Easter declaration, and about our response today to the central miracle of the Christian faith.

Literally thousands of times you have probably repeated the words: "For thine is the kingdom, and the power, and the glory." I doubt if we ever think very carefully about what we are saying. The phrase seems to round off the prayer—a kind of signing off to indicate that we're through and ready to begin the day's work, or perhaps to go to sleep. If you were to ask them, most people would say that they close the prayer this way because that is how Jesus finished it himself. But the evidence is that he didn't. In Luke's version of the Lord's Prayer this phrase does not occur, and if you look at the New English Bible translation you'll find it's not in Matthew either. A little footnote says: "Some witnesses add For thine is the kingdom and the power and the glory, for ever. Amen." That means that the most reliable manuscripts don't contain these words. Well, who were these "witnesses" who dared to make an addition to the prayer given by our Lord himself? The answer is simple. The early church adopted this prayer for use in their services of worship, and this was the way they ended when they said it together. It was almost a spontaneous outburst of praise and confidence. When they had repeated the words the Lord had taught them, it was as if they just couldn't help breaking out into triumphant praise. We must remember that these were people worshiping behind closed doors, in quarries, in caves, in catacombs. They knew that outside was the kingdom of imperial Rome, the power of the ancient religions and pagan philosophies, and the glorious symbols of Greco-Roman culture and art. So when they had prayed to the God and Father of Jesus Christ, they flung this challenge to the world they knew so well: "*Thine* is the kingdom, and the power, and the glory; so let it be."

What gave this tiny group of people the immense confidence that was to carry them through the fires of persecution to the very heart of the empire? What could bind together a Jewish teacher, an Egyptian slave, a Roman officer, a Greek merchant, a Macedonian widow, in the certainty that to their God belonged the kingdom, the power, and the glory, when nothing around them seemed to prove anything of the kind? Why should they lift such a defiant anthem to the skies when in fact their God was dead—crucified under Pontius Pilate? Put yourself back in these days when the empire of Rome was all-embracing,

89

when the power and the glory quite obviously belonged to the achievements of men or to the lurid underworld of demonic spirits, and you will know that these questions demand an answer. And there is only one answer that makes historical or practical sense. These people were this way, these people got this strength, these people could defy the world, because they believed that the Christ who was killed was alive again. Without a shadow of doubt this was the conviction that created and sustained the church. When Christians met, one would say, "Christ is risen," and the reply was, "He is risen indeed." When they gathered for worship, it was not only to remember his words and deeds but to meet with him. They knew that he was there. The first hymns they wrote celebrated the Resurrection. Their sacrament was no mere memorial rite but a communion with the living Lord. And the men who wrote the books we call the New Testament were all writing with the song of Resurrection in their hearts. This is why you cannot comb through the Gospels to extract material for a biography of Jesus Christ in modern terms, eliminating, demythologizing, reinterpreting, till you have something that will fit into our own framework of understanding. I am not for a moment saying that we must not bring modern critical judgment to bear upon these records, but simply that they cannot be understood if we ignore the fact that the writers really believed Jesus had risen from the dead.

The Lord's Prayer, then, was not for them simply a form of words given by their late teacher, Jesus of Nazareth. As such it was helpful, but not really new. Every phrase in it could be paralleled in the Old Testament and the prayers their rabbis taught. When they used this prayer it was already transformed by the spirit of the crucified and risen Lord. It was soaked in his blood. It glowed with his presence. The Father in heaven to whom it was addressed was the Father who had delivered them from evil by raising up Jesus from the dead.

Why is it that you and I can pray the Lord's Prayer without a flicker of lively expectation, just sending our thoughts along a familiar groove into a religious fog? Why is it that so many of our regular prayers are so dim that they could be described in T. S. Eliot's words as

> . . . a raid on the inarticulate
> With shabby equipment always deteriorating
> In the general mess of imprecision of feeling?

Isn't the real reason a lack of resonance of faith and impetus of love? I mean that when we have said the words, they seem to go trailing off into infinity instead of being orchestrated into the doxology of faith and winged by our love for the

91

Father in heaven. When Jesus used again and again the analogy of the child and his father, surely this is an important part of it. When the little boy rushes to his father and says, "Give me a tricycle," the whole force and reality of the prayer come from the enormous confidence and love that he has for his parent. At this stage in a happy family, Daddy is the one who can do anything, knows everything, and is altogether adorable (until teen-age sets in). Anything can be asked, and will be asked repeatedly—whether granted or not— for behind the child's request is the conviction that "thine is the kingdom, and the power, and the glory." Our Lord deliberately spoke of little children, for this is the kind of trust and confidence he expects us to have in the heavenly Father.

But now, you say, we are teen-agers (that is a more modest claim than to have come of age). We are not so sure about this omnipotent, omniscient Father in heaven any more. We can run our own lives. We can do for ourselves the things we used to leave to our God. We have broken out of the religious kindergarten and now the world is our oyster. "Ours is the kingdom, and the power, and the glory." Really? Then why pray at all? I think we are coming to the point where the choice between God and no-God is being thrust upon our generation exactly as it was in the past. At the moment many are living in that gray area where the instincts of ancestral religion are struggling with a secular world swept clean of God. The battle of beliefs and the uproar in theology are signs of "agonizing reappraisal" of religion. It is good for all of us to be forced to think again about what we say we believe and the words we have used. But when the tumult has died down, is there not still the basic question which has never been decided in any generation on any other terms than faith: Do we believe in this God whom Jesus represents—the Father in heaven whose is "the kingdom, and the power, and the glory"?

It was never easy. The Roman soldier, mesmerized by the kingdom and the power he saw in action all around him, the Athenian intellectual, skeptical about all religion and satisfied with the "glory that was Greece," were not pushovers for the gospel of a sovereign God whose gift of himself to the world meant a crucifixion and a resurrection. Yet there were those among them who heard it and believed. An Augustine, a Pascal, a Calvin, a Henry Drummond, a Schweitzer—these and thousands like them were men who had no innate propensity to believe. It is rubbish to talk of "ages of faith" as though there ever was a time when reflective men and women were not tormented by the most radical doubts. They never will be resolved by some new twist of logic or soul-shattering miracle performed before our eyes.

No God—that is your choice, not forced upon you by any weight of evidence. God—that is your choice, not forced upon you by any weight of evidence, except the contagion of those in whose lives we have caught a glimpse of the kingdom and the power and the glory.

The strongest contagion of this kind the world has ever known is without question the conviction that Jesus Christ rose from the dead. It is this that will give the resonance of faith and the impetus of love to these languid prayers. It is this that will make real to us the Father of whom he spoke. It is this that will continually restore to the church the joy and the freedom that are so often under cloud. The man or woman who underscores each prayer with the Resurrection doxology, who knows in each moment of triumph the humility, and in each moment of disaster the ultimate confidence that says: "Thine is the kingdom, and the power, and the glory," has known the presence of the risen Christ. Like the first Christians who inserted this refrain into the prayer the Lord had taught, they insert it into everything they say and do. For this is both the faith that holds through life and death, and the adoration that frees the soul for laughter and delight. God knows how desperate are the problems that confront us at this time, and how serious the decisions that weigh upon us all. But the missing note in so much

Christian argument and activity around us today is surely the ultimate gaiety of spirit that can throw open a window, like Pope John in the Vatican not long ago, and beam upon a snarling world the radiant belief that Christ is alive, that God's in his heaven, and that his spirit is at work in every corner of his creation. Argue, if you like, about the need for a doctine of the Trinity. I only know that there are times when I can do nothing else than cry out: "Glory be to the Father, and to the Son, and to the Holy Ghost."

I don't write like this because you are expecting a word of cheer, or because it's a beautiful spring day, or because the nation is surging with the spirit of celebration. I could not offer you the Resurrection doxology unless I could say just this to the one among you whose heart is heavy with anguish. There is no necessary connection between a date on the calendar and the spirit of radiant faith. One of my friends in the ministry in Scotland, who personifies the joy of this Christian conviction, lost his first child, an infant dropped on the stairway by a nurse, on Easter Day. And I could not offer you the Resurrection doxology unless I could also speak it in a village in Vietnam. I am not talking about a spirit of optimism, or about a God who shines forever out there in space like the sun beyond these threatening clouds. I am talking about a God who came here, about

95

Jesus Christ, who lived like us through storm and sunshine, who was hurt by what hurts us, who was crushed by the kingdom of evil, delivered to the powers of this world, and overwhelmed by the demonic glory of hell unleashed. He died. That was the moment when all prayers could cease, when the world was darkness and all life absurd. And on the third day God brought him back to life, and life has never been the same.

It was not a myth. It was Jesus. It was not a beautiful idea. It was Jesus, standing by an empty tomb and saying: *Mary.* It was Mary saying: *Master.* It was Mary telling the others, and the others telling their friends, and their friends telling the world. The Resurrection doxology is born into the hearts of people like you and me by the infection of a faith that is unbroken across two-thousand years. It is not shaken by any change in our ways of thought, or deflected by any invention of men. Surrounded by the threatening forces of the modern world, and taunted by the philosophies of despair and the cult of the absurd, we join the chorus of the church in heaven and on earth: "Thine is the kingdom, and the power, and the glory." For the living Christ is with us now, and his word is the same: "Peace I leave with you, my peace I give unto you: not as the world giveth, give I unto you. Let not your heart be troubled, neither let it be afraid."